SELLING
IN
CRISIS

Professional Selling Skills

Copyright (c) 2013 by: Adegoke Omotola

Printed in the Federal Republic of Nigeria by:
Medlantic Communications Ltd,
Tel: 0802 316 0320

ISBN: 9798646597480

First Printing 2009

For comments, enquiries or to place order:
Email: adegokeomotola@1stdegreeconsulting.net. Website: 1stdegreeconsulting.net

HOW TO CONTACT THE AUTHOR

Mr. Adegoke Omotola is the **CEO** of 1st Degree Consulting a company that is primarily engaged in management consulting. Training employees and captains of organizations in areas such as Customer Retention, Professional Selling and Marketing Skills, Leadership, Communication/Interpersonal Skills, Business Etiquette, Business Ethics amongst others nationwide. These services are tailored to suit the organisations needs as to build a robust and combustible impact.

All inquiries, invitations and comments should be directed to:

1st Degree Consulting
18, Michael Adekoya Street, Ilupeju, Lagos

For more information about special discount for bulk purchases, please contact:
Email: adegokeomotola@1stdegreeconsulting.net.
Tel No. 0802 223 1027
Website: 1stdegreeconsulting.net

TABLE OF CONTENTS

Qualities of a good Sales Person

Ten reasons why sales people fail

Other books by Adegoke Omotola

- Customer Retention

- Experiential Approach

Preface

This book is written for men and women who will not allow themselves to be bound down by psychological barriers and are determined to become robust and combustible as they overcome obstacles.

I give all the glory to God for the inspiration to write this book.

I appreciate the contributions of my lovely wife, Omoyemi and our beautiful daughters Layo and Bukunmi towards making this book a success.

I wish to say a big thank you as well to friends and family too numerous to mention.

Introduction

- What separates the successful salesperson from the other members of the sales community? Look at the basics – the simple stuff that sales professionals overlook from time to time. Things like the ability to listen carefully, respond correctly, and approach clients not as a sale but as people you want to know and help solve problems.

- These are the things to focus on in order to bring more value and visibility to your career. While they are common sense, these methods are often the first ones we forget to use.

- The fundamental skill required to get rich is to know what to sell and how to sell it.

What is Selling?

Understanding your customer's needs and fulfilling those needs.

Selling is the art of planting in the mind of another a motive which will induce favourable action.

Communication between you and your prospects to get them to open their wallets in exchange for your products and services.

Components of a Successful Sales Strategy

Preparation is fundamental.

Always remind your customers how great your product is and how much you value their business.

Embrace change- reinvent yourself.
Develop a resilient personality.
Follow up to build customer faith.

Starting Off

- Salesperson must have a pleasant look.

- Exchange greetings.

- Tell your name, organization, and purpose of visit

- Explain benefit of product or service.

- Get the prospect or Customer involved in the Sales Process

The customer as your partner.

It involves the ability to anticipate customers' needs even before they know they need it.

- Meet and exceed customers goals regularly.
- Identify customers' needs.
- Ask questions and listen.
- Keep making things happen.
- Deliver on promises.

Steps to successful Selling

Layout the groundwork.
-Knowledge
-Attitude.
-Techniques.

Approach and Relate
-Build a rapport.
-Appreciate the prospect for interest.

Make the presentation.
-Know the features.
-Sell the benefits.

What's in it for the customer?
-Sell the advantages.
-Why are you better than the competitor?

Overcome objections
-Turn No to Yes.

Closing the sale.
-Always be closing.

Suggest additional products.
-After initial decision has been made.

Follow up and make them customers for life.
-Contact customers after sale.
-Handle customer complaints promptly

Planning for Success

- A thorough product knowledge.

- Know your competition.

- Know company's strength and weaknesses.

- Know your industry.

- Know your customers well. (Research is the fuel of knowledge).

- Follow up, out of sight is out of mind.

To build customer base

- Continue to meet people to build a network.

- Solve customer challenges.

- Gain knowledge regularly of what is happening in you industry.

- Carve your niche, then market and sell to it aggressively.

- Build your interpersonal skills.

Relationship Selling

The salesperson with the most long- term (that is, loyal) customers wins. You win because you made it to the highest stage of a salesperson's career, which is relationship selling. You enjoy the rewards of your professional and personal relationships with customers. Years of meeting or exceeding customers' expectations will earn their loyalty.

Consultative Selling.

Consultative selling involves deeper questioning of the prospect, about organisational issues that can extend beyond the product itself.

- It is the process of involving the buyer in the selling proces and it is strongly based on questioning aimed at gainin useful information.

- Listening is very important in consultative selling without good listening skills the process o questioning is rendered totally pointless.

Suggestion Selling.

This can be described as encouraging your customer to buy more by making a definite suggestion for another product or service that they may need.

Whenever the sales person makes a suggestion of additional products, it increase the bottom line for that company or organisation.

Collaborative Selling

- It is the partnering between the customer and seller. Both organisations realise that their longer term success is predicated on both of them staying in business.

- We are currently in a period of restraint and cut backs. Sales volumes are down in almost all sectors and companies will be required to make tough business decisions to survive.

- There may be some opportunities where the buyer can be flexible in order to help the seller survive.

Brinkmanship Selling

Brinkmanship selling otherwise known as impromptu selling can be described as selling to a prospect within a short time frame, usually between 5-15 minutes to close the sale and make it happen.

You do not want to waste time presenting products or services that might not satisfy the prospect.

Courtship Selling

Courtship selling occurs in a situation where you sell to those that you are just starting a business relationship with and as more trust is earned the relationship gets better. The new buyers who do not yet qualify as long-term customers. Sometimes these new customers act like long-term customers.

Courtship selling is a blend of brinkmanship and relationship selling. Your challenge is to know which selling mode you need to use and when.

Online Selling Strategy

- Build Your Customer Avatar
- Grow Awareness & Visibility
- Drive Website Traffic
- Convert Traffic
- Increase Conversion Rate
- Increase Sales

If you want to increase sales, you must successfully increase awareness, traffic, and conversions. During crisis is the time to be visible in spite of social distancing by using platforms such as Zoom, LinkedIn, YouTube, Facebook, Instagram, Email Marketing etc. to reach your customers

Assets:

You need to invest into assets today that will produce returns tomorrow. The assets are top SEO rankings, social media followers, and email subscribers. If you have this, you can drive thousands of "free" and "organic" results. These results consist of thousands of impressions and clicks to your website. If you sell something great, this free traffic will turnover into sales.

Tips on Selling

- Customers want you to follow up.

- People buy from whom they can trust.

- Remember people's names.

- Carry out investigation on competitors.

- Don't manipulate your customer, educate your customer.

- Your product must be unique.

- You must continue to prospect.

- Don't knock your competitor.

- You must be highly motivated.

- Good personal hygiene.

Sources of Prospects.

- Referrals.
- Friends and relatives.
- Directories
- Trade shows/fair.
- Cold calls.
- Direct marketing.
- Networking.
- Newspapers.
- Radio/Tv.
- Internet.

Qualities of a good Sales Person.

- Physical fitness
- Courage.
- Product knowledge.
- Has capacity to listen.
- Building relationships.
- Good planning skills.
- Shows empathy.
- Persistence.
- Manages time well.
- Enthusiasm.
- Building trust.
- Ability to negotiate well.
- Ability to close a sale.

Ten reasons why sales people fail

- Over promise/ Under deliver.
- Promising things that you cannot deliver at all.
- Lack of product knowledge.
- Poor communication skills.
- Poor presentation skills.
- Failure to suggest alternatives.
- Poor networking skills.
- Inability to cope with rejection.
- Procrastination.
- Poor planning skills.

No matter who you are or how much you know, you will not succeed unless you are a salesman! You must sell your services. You must sell your knowledge. You must sell yourself. You must sell your personality.

References

1. The New Science of Selling and Persuasion. William T.Brooks. 2001.

2. The Enterpreneur's Guidebook Series 2001.

3. Essential Selling Skills. Todd Cohen 2008.

4. Customer Retention "An Experential Approach" Adegoke Omotola. 2010.

5. How to Sell Your Way Through Life. Napoleon Hill. 2010.